3,50

American Lives

Luisa Moreno

Heidi Moore

Heinemann Library
Chicago, Illinois

Designed by Q2A Creative

Printed in China by WKT Limited

10 09 08 07 06
10 9 8 7 6 5 4 3 2 1

Library of Congress Cataloging-in-Publication Data
Moore, Heidi, 1976-
Luisa Moreno / Heidi Moore.–1st ed.
    p. cm. -- (American lives)

Includes bibliographical references and index.
ISBN 1-4034-6978-4 (hc)–ISBN 1-4034-6985-7
    (pb)
1. Moreno, Luisa, d. 1992–Juvenile literature.
2. Women labor leaders–United States–Biography–
Juvenile literature. 3. Women labor union
members–United States–Biography–Juvenile
literature. I. Title. II. Series: American lives
(Heinemann Library (Firm))

HD6509.M64M66 2006
331.88'092–dc22

2005010100

Acknowledgments
The author and publishers are grateful to the
following for permission to reproduce copyright
material:

AP/Wide World Photos pp. **8**, **9**, **16**; Corbis pp. **20**
(Genevieve Naylor), **22**, **23**; Corbis/Bettmann pp. **4**,
11, **12**, **13**, **21**, **24**, **26**; Corbis/Hulton-Deutsch
Collection p. **17**; History San Jose p. **19**; Institute of
Texan Cultures p. **15**; Library of Congress pp. **6**, **14**,
25; Pomona Public Library/The Frasher Foto
Postcard Collection p. **18** (Burton Frasher);
Southern California Library for Social Studies and
Research pp. **5**, **7**, **27**, **28**, **29**; Underwood Archives
p. **10**.

The cover portrait of Luisa Moreno is reproduced
with permission of the Southern California Library
for Social Studies and Research.

Every effort has been made to contact copyright
holders of any material reproduced in this book.
Any omissions will be rectified in subsequent
printings if notice is given to the publisher.

Some words are shown in bold, **like this**. You can
find out what they mean by looking in the glossary.

Contents

A Guatemalan Girl

A girl named Blanca Rosa Lopez Rodriguez was growing up in Guatemala in the early 1900s. Guatemala is a country in Central America. Blanca came from a wealthy family, but many people in her country were poor.

When she was about twenty, she moved to the United States. She saw the bad conditions facing many workers in **sweatshops** and on farms. She decided to fight for their rights. Blanca changed her name to Luisa Moreno and became an **activist**.

These garment workers protested their working conditions in New York, in 1933.

The Life of Luisa Moreno

1907	1916	1920s	1928	1929
Born on August 30, 1907 in Guatemala	*Went to school in California*	*Returned to Guatemala (exact date unknown)*	*Moved to New York City*	*Went to work in New York factory*

Luisa Moreno's campaigning helped thousands of workers in the United States.

Luisa Moreno was an important **Latin-American** leader in the United States. She became the first Latin-American vice president of a major **labor union**. She helped thousands of workers across the country fight for better working conditions. With her help, many workers succeeded in getting better pay, shorter working hours, and fairer treatment.

1930	1934	1941	1949	1992
Joined cafeteria strike in New York	*Joined CIO*	*Became vice president of UCAPAWA*	*Left the United States*	*Died in Guatemala on November 4*

Growing Up

Here is an old picture of Guatemala at the time Luisa was growing up there.

Blanca Rosa Lopez Rodriguez was born on August 30, 1907, in Guatemala City, Guatemala. Her parents were a wealthy couple named Ernesto Rodriguez and Alicia Lopez Rodriguez.

In 1916, Blanca moved to the United States with her parents. They moved there so Blanca could go to the College of the Holy Name in Oakland, California. This school was not a college the way we think of one today. It was a junior high and high school for girls. Blanca was a boarding student, which means that she lived at the college.

After she graduated, she and her family went back to Guatemala. There, while still a teenager, she formed *La Sociedad Gabriela Mistral* (The Gabriela Mistral Society). The society fought for educational rights for women. At that time Guatemalan women were not allowed to attend university. The group fought for, and won, the right for women to attend universities.

This is a picture of Luisa as a young woman.

On Her Own

Even though she fought for the right for women to go to university, Blanca did not go herself. Instead, she moved to Mexico to write poetry and newspaper articles. She used her articles to fight for **civil rights**. She believed that everyone should be treated equally under the law.

In 1927, Luisa met the famous Mexican artist Diego Rivera, who was also interested in workers' rights. Here, Rivera works on "The Detroit Industry Murals" at The Detroit Institute of Art in 1932. The work was completed in 1933.

Diego Rivera painted this mural in 1928.

Blanca changed her name to Luisa Moreno in honor of a famous Mexican **labor** organizer named Luis Moreno. He also felt that all people should be treated fairly. She was known by this new name for the rest of her life.

Her parents were upset about her decision to become an **activist**. They believed she should not spend her life working with poor people. But Luisa thought all people should have the same rights no matter where they were born or who their parents were.

Back to America

In 1927 Luisa married a Mexican artist named Miguel Angel de Leon. The next year they both **immigrated** to the United States. They moved to New York City. That year she gave birth to a daughter they named Mytyl.

In 1929 the country entered a difficult period called the **Great Depression**. Many people were out of work. Luisa's husband could not find work either. So she went to work at a **garment** factory in Spanish Harlem, an area of New York City with many Spanish-speaking immigrants.

This is a New York garment factory in 1920, similar to the one Luisa worked in. It was also a sweatshop.

During the Depression men waited in line for hours, hoping to find work.

The factory was a **sweatshop**. Workers worked long hours for very little pay. The factory bosses forced them to work even when injured. Luisa had to run her sewing machine for hours without a break. She became angry about the bad working conditions and decided to do something about it. She formed a garment workers' **union** called *Liga de Costureras*. This is Spanish for "Union of Garment Workers". The union wanted to help workers gain rights such as higher pay, better hours, and safer working conditions.

Going on Strike

These workers are on strike. They are picketing.

In 1930 Luisa took a job at a cafeteria in New York. Workers there were upset about working long hours for little pay, so they went on **strike**. That means they refused to go to work. They did that to force their bosses to listen to their complaints.

Luisa decided to strike with them. But police officers tried to keep her and the other striking workers from **picketing**. Picketing means marching in the street with signs that explain the reasons for the strike. Luisa tried to stand up to the police, but they grabbed her and hit her. This unfair treatment made her even angrier.

That same year she joined the **Communist Party** in New York. The party wanted to end **segregation** in public places such as schools and swimming pools. Segregation is when one group of people is kept separate from another group. Segregation happens because of **discrimination**. The Communists wanted to fight discrimination. They wanted equal rights for women and **Latin Americans**.

Members of the Communist Party march in New York City in 1935.

On the Move

In the 1930s Luisa became a **labor** organizer for the **American Federation of Labor (AFL)**. She moved from state to state, helping workers form **unions** to fight for fair pay and better working conditions. She spent time in Louisiana, Florida, Pennsylvania, and Texas, helping factory workers.

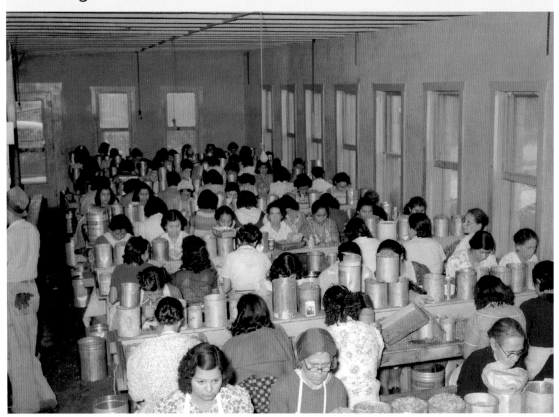

Working conditions in factories were often crowded.

Emma Tenayuca was a strong labor leader like Luisa.

One of her most important battles for workers' rights took place in San Antonio, Texas. There, she worked with Texan labor organizer Emma Tenayuca to organize women at a pecan factory. Together the women led a **strike** at the Southern Pecan Shelling Company. During the strike, thousands of workers at more than 130 factories spoke out against a pay cut.

Low Pay:

In Texas in the 1930s, field workers picked beets, cabbage, corn, and other vegetables for only 50 cents a day. At the time, the average pay for workers was about $4 a day.

A Union Leader

Jobless people wait in line for a free meal in New York, 1932.

By 1934 Luisa had joined the **Congress of Industrial Organizations (CIO)**, a group of **unions** that joined together to organize unskilled workers. She was the first **Latin-American** woman to join the California CIO.

In November of 1936, she attended a **labor** organization meeting in Tampa, Florida. The goals of the meeting were to create an international union of food and farm workers. But some members were not happy with how things were going at the meeting. They believed the leaders were not listening to their ideas. So they decided to form a separate union. They called it the **United Cannery, Agricultural, Packing, and Allied Workers of America (UCAPAWA)**. Luisa would become an important leader of this new union.

This 1931 photo of a San Diego cannery shows what working conditions were like at the time.

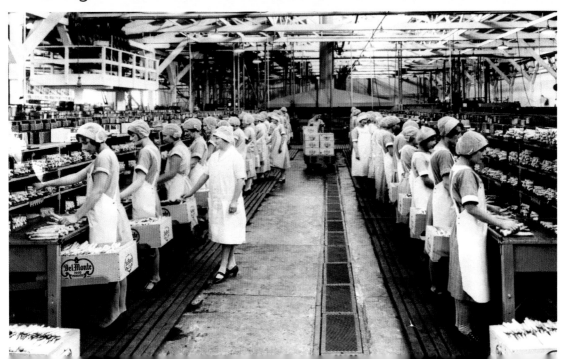

Spanish-Speaking Congress

In 1937 Luisa and her husband Miguel **divorced**. She moved with her daughter Mytyl to San Diego to help **UCAPAWA** organize workers in tuna factories. These **cannery** workers spent long hours in **sweatshop** conditions. She wanted to help them form **unions**.

Luisa traveled to Los Angeles in order to organize *El Congreso de Pueblos Que Hablan Espanol.*

HISTORIC OLVERA STREET IN SHADOW OF CITY HALL LOS ANGELES, CALIFORNIA

In 1939, working as an international representative of UCAPAWA, Moreno helped organize a group called *El Congreso de Pueblos Que Hablan Español* (The Congress of Spanish-Speaking Peoples). They wanted to end **segregation** in public places, in schools, and in the workplace. This was the first conference to bring together unions and other groups to fight for **Latin-American** rights.

Luisa helped organize events like this one.

As a leader, Luisa believed in sharing responsibility. At the Congress, she worked with Mexican **labor** organizer Josefina Fierro de Bright. Josefina helped bring people from across the country to the meeting.

OFFICIAL PROGRAM

GRAND BALL

SPONSORED BY

Cannery Workers Union

of Santa Clara County, Local 20852

of the

A. F. of L.

◆

CIVIC AUDITORIUM, SAN JOSE

Saturday, November 27, 1937

◆

Valuable Door Prizes

MUSIC BY ELWOOD HART'S ORCHESTRA

11

Strength in Numbers:

The United Cannery, Agricultural, Packing, and Allied Workers of America was a union group founded in 1937. Many of its members were women, Latin Americans, and African Americans. In 1944 UCAPAWA became the Food, Tobacco, Agricultural, and Allied Workers of America (FTA).

The California Whirlwind

These women in a New Hampshire cannery sorted cranberries.

In 1941 the United States entered World War II. The country was at war until 1945. At the time, Luisa was living in San Diego, California. San Diego was an important center of production during the war because it had a lot of factories.

Luisa became international vice president of **UCAPAWA** in 1941. She was vice president until 1947. During that time, she worked with many different **unions** in the San Diego area. She fought for equal rights for **Latin-American** workers in factories and on farms. In 1945 she won an important battle at Pacific Grape Products, a large **cannery** in California. She helped workers there get a fair contract with paid holidays, time off for illness, and twice the normal pay on Sundays and holidays.

Her successes in California earned her the nickname the "California **Whirlwind**" because she was strong like a whirlwind and seemed to knock down any obstacles in her path.

Luisa was also able to help many foreign-born workers, like these, to stay in the country and keep their jobs.

Making a Difference

Between 1938 and 1947, Luisa helped thousands of farm and factory workers form **unions**. She organized sugar beet workers in Colorado. She helped factory workers in a chili **cannery** in San Diego, California. She also helped California walnut farmers. Luisa was a strong leader in part because she was **bilingual**. She could speak Spanish with the workers and English with their bosses.

Some Mexican farm workers protest from the back of a truck during a strike.

Luisa Wrote this Saying for UCAPAWA:

*"An injury to one is an injury to all." This means that when one person is hurt, everyone is hurt. She wrote this because of all the injuries that happened in **sweatshops**. She wanted factories to be safe places to work.*

As a leader of **UCAPAWA**, Luisa helped union members fight for higher pay, better working conditions, and equal pay for their work. Equal pay was important because some companies **discriminated** against women and **Latin Americans** by paying them less money for the same amount of work.

These Mexican workers in Minnesota have been cutting sugar beet.

Second Marriage

Around the time she was 40 years old, Luisa met a U.S. Navy sailor named Gray Bemis. They married on February 1, 1947. Luisa stopped traveling around the country and settled down with her new husband.

Together, they moved into an apartment near the beach in San Diego. There, Luisa had a much quieter life. She wrote a book about her **labor** activities. She also taught a class at the California Labor School in nearby Los Angeles. The class was called "Mexican-Americans and the Fight for **Civil Rights**."

Luisa wrote articles on a typewriter like this one.

This is San Diego, where Luisa lived with her second husband, Gray Bemis.

In 1949 they built a small red house in San Diego. There, Luisa wrote newspaper articles on her black Remington typewriter. She loved spending time in the garden.

Forced To Leave

The late 1940s were a hard time for **unions.** Certain people in the government thought unions were **Communist.** Many unions had members who belonged to the Communist party at some point, but most unions were not Communist organizations. At the time, some people in the government were afraid of Communists taking over the country and changing the political system.

Soon the government accused Luisa of being a Communist. She had to testify, or speak in court, in 1948. The next year, the government decided she should be **deported.** Luisa had never become a citizen of the United States. Even though she had lived here for years, the government could force her to leave the country.

The House Un-American Activities Commission questions Luisa.

This picture shows Luisa sometime after she was deported.

Before she left she burned a lot of photos and personal records. She was afraid the government would use them to arrest or deport her friends and family. Unfortunately, a lot of early **labor** history was lost forever.

Luisa Moreno Bemis left the United States forever in 1950. Her husband Gray went with her.

Remembering Luisa Moreno

After leaving the United States, Luisa and Gray drove to Mexico. They lived there for several years until Gray died in 1960. Luisa, saddened by his death, moved to Cuba. In the late 1970s, her health became worse. She moved back to Guatemala to live with her brother. On November 4, 1992, Luisa died in the country where she had been born.

Luisa never came back to the United States, but her fight for **civil rights** went on. She had helped thousands of workers form **unions**. Now they had the power to fight for better pay, safer working conditions, and equality.

Luisa later in life.

Her daughter Mytyl Glomboske also went on to fight for workers' rights. She once said, "I think of my mother and she is in my heart when I participate for the struggle for justice."

A sign over the door to Luisa's house in San Diego read, "We are created to serve others."

Luisa (right) sits with her daughter, Mytyl.

Glossary

activist   person who takes action to support a cause

American Federation of Labor (AFL)   group of labor unions, started in 1886

bilingual   able to speak two languages

cannery   factory where workers pack fruits, vegetables, or other foods in cans

civil rights   fair and equal treatment for everyone

Communist Party   group that believes in the equal sharing of property

Congress of Industrial Organizations (CIO) group of labor unions that broke off from the AFL in 1935

deported   forced to leave a country

discrimination   unfair treatment toward a group of people

divorced   legal ending of a marriage

garment   piece of clothing

Great Depression   period from 1929 to 1933 when many people were out of work

immigrant   person born in another country

immigrated   came to a country

labor   work, especially by hand

Latin American   person from Mexico, Central America, South America, or the islands of the West Indies

picketing   standing outside a workplace with signs to protest something

segregation   unfairly separate a group of people

strike   stop working to protest something, usually unfair treatment

sweatshop   place where workers work long hours for little pay, often under bad or unsafe conditions

union   group that fights for workers' rights and better working conditions for its members

United Cannery, Agricultural, Packing, and Allied Workers of America (UCAPAWA)   labor union that split off from the CIO in 1937

whirlwind   forceful, swirling movement of air

Places to Visit

Embassy Auditorium
851 South Grand Avenue
Los Angeles, California
This was the site of several union meetings (of cannery and packing workers) organized by Luisa Moreno and Josefina Fierro de Bright.

House where Luisa lived in the 1940s
6426 Medio Drive
San Diego, California

Index